Immigration

DEBATING
THE ISSUES

Immigration

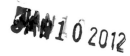
Marshall Cavendish
Benchmark
New York

RUTH
BJORKLUND

Published by Marshall Cavendish Benchmark
An imprint of Marshall Cavendish Corporation

Other Marshall Cavendish Offices:
Marshall Cavendish International (Asia) Private Limited, 1 New Industrial Road, Singapore 536196 •
Marshall Cavendish International (Thailand) Co Ltd. 253 Asoke, 12th Flr, Sukhumvit 21 Road, Klongtoey
Nua, Wattana, Bangkok 10110, Thailand • Marshall Cavendish (Malaysia) Sdn Bhd, Times Subang, Lot 46,
Subang Hi-Tech Industrial Park, Batu Tiga, 40000 Shah Alam, Selangor Darul Ehsan, Malaysia

Marshall Cavendish is a trademark of Times Publishing Limited

All websites were available and accurate when this book was sent to press.

Library of Congress Cataloging-in-Publication Data

Bjorklund, Ruth.
Immigration / Ruth Bjorklund.
p. cm. — (Debating the issues)
Includes bibliographical references and index.
ISBN 978-0-7614-4973-7 — ISBN 978-1-60870-665-5 (ebook)
1. United States—Emigration and immigration—Juvenile literature. I. Title.
JV6465.B46 2012
325.73—dc22
2010039510

Editor: Peter Mavrikis
Publisher: Michelle Bisson
Art Director: Anahid Hamparian
Series design by Sonia Chaghatzbanian

Photo research by Alison Morretta

Printed in Malaysia (T)
135642

Table of Contents

Chapter 1

"**America** is open to receive not only the Opulent and respectable Stranger, but the oppressed and persecuted of all Nations And Religions; whom we shall welcome to a participation of all our rights and privileges, if by decency and propriety of conduct they appear to merit the enjoyment." This declaration that the new nation would open its doors to anyone of good character was made by George Washington, the first president of the United States. Throughout its history, many think that America's strength and success has come from being a nation of **immigrants**. More recently, President Barack Obama has said, "We know that our patchwork heritage is a strength, not a weakness. . . . We are shaped by every language and culture, drawn from every end of this Earth. . . ." and "Part of America's genius has always been its ability to absorb newcomers, to forge a national identity out of the disparate lot that arrived on our shores." Yet many believe that immigration is no longer a benefit to society and in fact stands in the way of American growth and prosperity. Senator Charles Schumer of New York says that our immigration system is broken. Reform is necessary. In a speech before Congress he said, "Any reformed

The 305-foot (93-meter) copper statue in New York harbor named "Liberty Enlightening the World" was a gift from France to the United States in recognition of American democracy.

immigration system must be successful in encouraging the next Albert Einstein to emigrate permanently to the United States while, at the same time, discouraging underpaid, temporary workers from taking jobs that could and should be filled by qualified American workers."

In 1908, the English playwright Israel Zangwill had a success in America with his play *The Melting Pot*. It portrayed people who had come to America from all over the world and "melted" together into a

Many American cities, such as New York, Boston, San Francisco, and Seattle, have thriving "Chinatowns" where generations of Asian immigrants have come to live and work.

common culture. However, the newcomers and those already living in the country shared the same western European culture, religion, and values. Today immigrants come from so many foreign lands that many say America is no longer a melting pot but a "salad bowl," where the individual "ingredients" simply live side by side and do not blend in. Many believe that it is too easy for foreign-born immigrants to set themselves apart in like-minded communities on the basis of race, religion, or ethnic group. They do not make an effort to learn English and are less inclined to shed their native culture and adopt a more American way of life. Detractors of immigration contend that immigrants isolated in their own small communities will fail to achieve the success they came to America for and eventually may harm the whole of American society.

Immigration Patterns

America was first settled by colonists from England, France, Spain, and the Netherlands. The first settlers arrived in the New World and found enormous tracts of arable land and abundant natural resources. Though most came with money, they lacked the human resources that were critical to expanding their claims and benefiting from their lands. So the settlers turned to their countrymen and women and encouraged them to immigrate to America with promises of prosperity, freedom, and a new way of life.

From the seventeenth century to the early part of the nineteenth, settlers came mostly from France, England, Scotland, Wales, and Northern

This painting shows Jamestown colonists enthusiastically welcoming new immigrants who have come to America to escape religious persecution and seek their fortune.

Ireland. Jewish families from the Netherlands and Poland were also part of the early wave. Most were poor and sought cheap farmland. Many arrived as indentured servants: that is, people who borrowed from others for their ship's passage and had to work off the debt. Eventually, they paid for their freedom and were able to farm land of their own.

In the early part of the nineteenth century, Napoléon, the emperor of France, went to war with several European nations, and in 1815, when the wars ended, many former British and European soldiers immigrated to America. During the same period, New York City had become an important port, and the Northeast had begun to industrialize. The completion of the construction of the Erie Canal, in upstate New York, which opened up areas in the Midwest, added to the lure of the New World. Between 1820 and the 1880s, approximately 15 million Europeans took advantage of new opportunities in the United

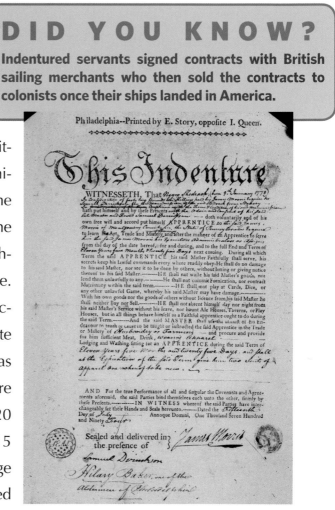

DID YOU KNOW?
Indentured servants signed contracts with British sailing merchants who then sold the contracts to colonists once their ships landed in America.

The typical term of a contract of indenture was seven years of unpaid labor.

States and immigrated to New York, Boston, Philadelphia, and the fertile farmlands of the Midwest.

Immigrants tended to live in communities with others from their home countries. The Midwest was settled largely by immigrants from Sweden, Norway, Denmark, and Germany. Protestant Europeans remained in the largest cities—New York, Philadelphia, and Boston. Prior to the start of the Civil War in 1861, many Irish Roman Catholics immigrated to New York and Boston. Chinese men also came looking for work.

Until the Civil War, immigrants arrived by sailing ship, but after the war, tech-

> # DID YOU KNOW?
> **During the American Civil War, Chinese immigrants enlisted and fought in the armies and navies of both the North and the South.**

nology had advanced, and large ships powered by steam engines were able to transport a whole new wave of immigrants. Around the turn of the twentieth century, nearly 25 million immigrants arrived—Italians, Greeks, Hungarians, Poles, and others from eastern Europe, including Jews. These new settlers moved to the cities, where they found work in the steel, coal, and automobile manufacturing industries, in textile mills, and in the garment trade.

In the era after World War II, many people left the war-torn parts of Europe for America, including displaced persons, Jewish **refugees**, war brides, and political **asylum** seekers from Russia and eastern Europe. Later in the twentieth century, immigrants included many Asians, Mexicans, and Latin Americans, as well as refugees from wars in Southeast

Asia and political asylum seekers from Cuba, Iran, Bosnia, Somalia, and other areas suffering from persecution and conflict.

Immigration Laws

The first U.S. immigration law was the Naturalization Act of 1790, which allowed any "free white person" of "good moral character" who had lived in the United States for at least two years to apply for citizenship. The law also stated that children born outside the country to parents who are U.S. citizens were immediately considered citizens. In 1798, as the United States anticipated war with France, Congress passed four laws collectively called the Alien and Sedition Acts. The first, the Naturalization Act, extended the residency period of **aliens** seeking citizenship from five to fourteen years. The second, the Alien Act, authorized the president to **deport** anyone "dangerous to the peace and safety of the United States." The third, the Alien Enemies Act, empowered the president to arrest, jail, and deport aliens from a country with which the United States was at war. The fourth, the Sedition Act, provided that any persons who wrote or published anything "treasonous" against the government could be fined and jailed.

When the U.S. Constitution was drafted, it made a concession to the southern states and allowed them to "import" African slaves. In 1808 the United States banned the importation of slaves. In 1819 a law was passed requiring a ship's captain to carry a list (or manifest) of everyone on board. By the middle of the nineteenth century, the government began to further limit who could immigrate. In 1865 Congress allowed

On the eve of World War II, Jewish refugees, such as these children greeting the Statue of Liberty, sought asylum in the United States.

temporary contract workers, but twenty years later it reversed the law. Later the Immigration Act of 1875 excluded convicts, prostitutes, indentured servants, and Chinese persons from entering the United States. Chinese laborers had been instrumental in building the transcontinental railroad, but once it was complete, many Americans feared that the Chinese workers would take over their jobs and work for less pay. In 1882, responding to the pressure, Congress passed the Chinese Exclusion Act, which halted Chinese immigration to the United States for ten years. In 1891, the first government agency was established to oversee immigration, and additional rulings were handed down excluding entry to poor people, polygamists, the insane, and anyone with a contagious disease. In 1903 and 1907, more groups of people were excluded, including people with mental or physical disabilities, epileptics, children under sixteen, "professional" beggars, and anarchists.

By the beginning of the twentieth century, many immigrants came via ship to the Pacific Coast seeking entry into the United States. In 1910 Angel Island, in California, was established as a customs port and became known as the Ellis Island of the West. In 1913 California passed the Alien Land Law, which barred noncitizens from owning land. The U.S. Congress continued to pass more immigration laws aimed at non-European immigrants. In 1917 it required all immigrants over the age of sixteen to take a literacy test. An immigrant needed to be able to read forty words in his or her own native language. However, as Asian immigrants read characters and not words, this test was a means of denying them entry.

A TALE OF TWO ISLANDS: EAST AND WEST

In 1890 a fort on a small island in New York harbor became the site of the first immigration station in the United States. Before then, immigrants seeking entry to the United States requested permission from individual states, but President Benjamin Harrison signed a document making immigration a federal responsibility. On January 2, 1892, a fifteen-year-old Irish girl named Annie Moore was the first immigrant to be processed at the Ellis Island immigration station. For the next sixty-two years, 12 million immigrants passed through the station gates. The majority of immigrants were European, as were the settlers already in America. For some, Ellis Island was an "island of tears," but most immigrants spent only a few hours having their paperwork processed by the Bureau of Immigration. As more people arrived, immigration practices changed. First- and second-class passengers on the steamships coming into the harbor were inspected on board. Only those in

A statue of Annie Moore and her two brothers commemorates their departure from Ireland to join their immigrant parents in New York. After twelve days in steerage, Annie was the first person to be admitted to the United States through the Ellis Island immigration station.

third and steerage class were processed on Ellis Island, and inspectors needed to assess whether or not the newcomers were undesirable. Doctors with the U.S. Public Health Service also did inspections and grew adept at performing "six-second physicals" to determine an immigrant's health. Only 2 percent of the arriving immigrants were turned away. After World War II, Ellis Island was used as a prison to detain suspected enemies of the state. Once the prisoners were deported, the Ellis Island immigration station reopened. It did not close until 1954. It is now a museum and part of the Ellis Island–Statue of Liberty National Monument.

In 1910 the doors opened to the Angel Island immigration station, located on an isolated island near San Francisco, California. Intended to guard the "western gate" of the United States, this "Ellis Island of the West" was built as a way of keeping out Chinese and other Asian immigrants. In 1849 word spread to China that there was a gold rush in California. Most Chinese were very poor, and so with the hope of finding gold, they left their homes and traveled across the Pacific. American gold miners, meanwhile, were not happy with the arrival of the Chinese. Legislators quickly passed laws banning the Chinese from the mines.

Without the prospect of gold and with no money to return home, the Chinese were desperate. The railroad companies took advantage of their poverty and hopelessness and hired them for very little pay. When the transnational railroad was completed, the Chinese were again out of work. The economy was in a downturn, and many Americans feared that the continuous flow of cheap Chinese labor would cause wages to sink. Lawmakers responded to the urging of those who favored immigration restriction with the Chinese Exclusion Act of 1882. In 1905, construction began on Angel Island to enforce the exclusion act and detain immigrants, especially Asians. Japanese immigrants were also unwelcome as many Americans felt threatened by the Japanese skill at farming. Responding to the outcry of California citizens, the United States passed the Immigration Act of 1924, which generally banned the Japanese from immigrating.

Immigrants at Ellis Island were subjected to quick health screenings before being allowed to enter the United States.

Until 1940 Angel Island processed more than a million immigrants from nearly ninety countries. Approximately 400,000 Asians, mostly Chinese and Japanese, were detained, and many were deported. Many of the Asian immigrants were detained for two or three weeks; some were kept for months or even years.

In 1997 the Angel Island immigration station became a National Historic Landmark.

In between harsh interrogation sessions, Chinese and Japanese detainees etched messages and poems on the walls of their barracks on Angel Island.

Between 1910 and 1940 U.S. immigration officials asked obscure trick questions in order to deport countless Chinese and Japanese immigrants. The government abandoned the Angel Island administration building after it caught fire in 1940, but it has been restored.

In 1921 the first immigration **quota** was enacted. The act limited immigration to 350,000 people annually from Europe and capped the number of persons from any one country to 3 percent of its representation in the 1910 census. Thus, immigration from southern and eastern Europe was largely curtailed. The Immigration Act of 1924 limited immigration to 165,000 people each year and contained an act called the National Origins Act, which lowered the 3 percent cap on nationalities to 2 percent and based its percentages on the 1890 census and thus

> ## DID YOU KNOW?
>
> In 1917 President Woodrow Wilson issued a proclamation ordering detention at Angel Island of all alien men over the age of fourteen from Germany, Austria, and Hungary. Later, in 1918, the order was extended to include all alien women over the age of fourteen who were born in those countries.

effectively eliminated Asians from immigrating. The U.S. Border Patrol was also established in 1924.

The National Origins Act of 1929 lowered the limit to 150,000 immigrants per year and allowed northern and western Europeans to make up 70 percent of the total and southern and eastern Europeans 30 percent. During World War II, with a serious shortage of low-wage workers, Congress allowed Mexicans and other Latin Americans to enter the country on a temporary basis and work in agriculture or factories. Also during the war, in recognition of China becoming a U.S. ally against Japan, the United States passed the Act to Repeal the Chinese Exclusion Acts, known as the Magnuson Act of 1943. The act allowed some Chinese to become **naturalized citizens**, but it also set a quota of 105 **visas** per year for Chinese immigrants. Wars were also responsible for the War Brides Act, the G.I. Fiancée Act, the Displaced Persons Act, the Refugee Relief Act of 1953, and the Hungarian Relief Act of 1956. These laws allowed entry for foreign-born spouses, children, and fiancées of soldiers and granted refuge and asylum to hundreds of thousands of people fleeing oppression in the aftermath of war.

In 1952 Congress passed a comprehensive immigration law called the Immigration and Nationality Act. It eliminated restrictions against Asians becoming naturalized citizens. It also set up a quota system favorable to persons who have valuable skills or professions and to family reunification. Additional rules defined deportation and exclusions based on political grounds (such as refusing entry to former Nazis).

In 1965 Congress enacted the Immigration and Nationality Act, which replaced the national origins quotas with a mostly family-based quota system, giving preferences to citizens who want family members to immigrate. By 1970, 8 million people had immigrated to the United States; nearly half were from Asia, and the other half were from Mexico. In 1980 Congress enacted the Refugee Act, which separated refugees from other immigrants and allowed refugees to come to the United States to avoid persecution on the basis of race, religion, nationality, or political beliefs. Quotas would be set every year by the president and could be increased at any time in an emergency.

Legislation involving illegal immigrants was first addressed in the Immigration Reform and Control Act of 1986. With this law, persons who had entered the country illegally and had lived in the country for at least four years could apply for citizenship. At the same time, the law called for stricter penalties and fines for employers who hired illegal workers.

In the 1990s, fear began to play a greater role in immigration legislation. The World Trade Center in New York City was bombed by foreign-born terrorists in 1993. When a group of American terrorists

After Socialists took control of Cuba, the United States passed the Cuban Adjustment Act of 1966, which granted nearly all Cuban immigrants the status of political refugees and the opportunity to become citizens one year after arrival. More than 200,000 asylum seekers fled Cuba by boat.

bombed a federal office building in Oklahoma City in 1995, citizens became increasingly uneasy about terrorism on American soil. Public sentiment demanded a response from the federal government. So in 1996 the Illegal Immigration Reform and Immigrant Responsibility Act became law, giving power to the Immigration and Naturalization Service—now known as the U.S. Citizenship and Immigration Services

(USCIS)—to quickly deport immigrants who had committed minor offenses. President Bill Clinton also signed the Antiterrorism and Effective Death Penalty Act, which said that legal nonresidents who had committed crimes and were punished with jail sentences longer than one year would automatically be deported.

After the terrorist attacks on September 11, 2001, Congress focused on strengthening immigration enforcement, reforming immigration laws, and securing the nation's borders. At the time, the secretary of state, Colin Powell, declared that the attacks had "fundamentally changed our view of the openness of our society." In 2002 Congress created the **Department of Homeland Security** (DHS), which took over and reorganized various immigration agencies and increased the number of immigration agents, investigators, and persons working in immigration detention centers.

Since the DHS was formed, there have been several attempts by lawmakers to address immigration reform. Included in the topics of concern are immigration quotas, illegal immigration, border security costs, locations of increased enforcement measures, detention procedures, deportation rules, **amnesty** for illegal immigrants, guest worker programs, workplace raids, English requirements, fines, and employer penalties. As late as 2011, no comprehensive reform bills were passed by Congress.

WHAT DO YOU THINK?

Europeans were the earliest immigrants and settlers in the United States. In later immigration waves, people from non-European countries arrived. State some of the reasons each group had for immigrating and highlight their different aims, if any.

How have immigration laws changed over the past one hundred years?

Have Americans' attitudes toward immigration changed? If so, how?

Do you think that deportation of legal residents who have committed serious crimes is reasonable?

Chapter 2

As the United States developed into an economic world power, the growth of new businesses, industries, farm production, and other enterprises expanded beyond the ability of the nation's workers to keep up with demand. The American economy had always been eager for new workers, especially low-wage workers willing to perform strenuous, distasteful, or difficult tasks. As the economy's need for labor grew, immigrants historically arrived to fill these jobs. Their efforts supported America's massive economic achievements. Although immigrant workers played such a vital role in the development of the nation, in light of new technology and changes in the global economy, many now say that immigrant workers are no longer needed.

Jobs and Wages

Until the twentieth century, the U.S. economy needed unskilled laborers for agriculture and other labor-intensive jobs such as working on railroad, highway, and other construction projects, in mines and mills, and on assembly lines. The more the country became industrialized, the more factories needed workers. Businesses welcomed immigrant workers because people from foreign countries did not make demands on their new American employers.

A roadway sign near the Mexican–U.S. border warns drivers to be alert for illegal immigrants who may suddenly emerge from their hideouts in the desert.

By the middle of the twentieth century, industry grew more technically advanced, and businesses developed a need for a better-trained,

more highly skilled labor force. In 2000, 69 percent of all adult immigrants had no profession, vocational skill, or job. More than a third of adult immigrants had not graduated from high school.

Agriculture remained the largest industry that employed unskilled

After Chinese immigrants were banned from the mines during the California gold rush, many turned to low-wage work, such as in this West Coast cannery.

laborers, but the number of jobs steadily decreased. Food production became more technical and advanced in its practices and thus required fewer unskilled workers. In 1900, 41 percent of the population was employed in agriculture. By 2000, that percentage had dropped to less than 2 percent.

Immigration laws passed in 1965 gave preference to people who were relatives of immigrants already in the United States. Immigrants seeking to join their naturalized families tended to have the same level of education and similar lack of vocational and technical skills. By 2007 foreign-born immigrants made up 48 percent of workers without high school educations. Irwin Kirsch, director of the

Manufacturing jobs considered dangerous and undesirable, such as meat-cutting or fish canning, have been traditionally performed by unskilled immigrant workers.

Center for Global Assessment, said, "Half of the U.S. population growth into the next decade is expected to come from new immigrants. . . . While immigrants come from diverse backgrounds with varying levels of education, we should recognize that 34 percent of new immigrants arrive without a high school diploma, and of those, 80 percent cannot speak English well, if at all." As demand for unskilled labor decreases, competition between immigrant workers and low-wage native-born workers is intensified. Today the United States grants approximately 5,000 **green cards** each year to low-wage immigrant workers. A green card (so called because it was originally green) is the nickname for a **Permanent Resident Card** (formerly called an Alien Registration Receipt Card), a photo identification card that proves an immigrant may live per-

manently in the country. Employers not only pay undocumented immigrants less money, they deny them most employee benefits, such as sick leave, vacation time, and health insurance. This policy keeps profits high and wages low, and the competition for job leads to a reduction in wages and benefits for native-born citizens.

> ## DID YOU KNOW?
> If a holder of a Permanent Resident Card leaves the United States, he or she must return within one year to maintain it.

Highly prized "green cards" allow immigrants to work legally in the United States. Many believe that comes at the expense of native-born workers who would be paid higher wages.

One of the most common arguments in favor of foreign-born workers is that they are willing and able to take jobs that native-born workers do not want to do, including jobs in construction, meatpacking, food service, landscaping, and janitorial and domestic service. Yet a 2007 Census Bureau community survey showed that 65 percent of meatpackers, 68 percent of construction workers, 73 percent of dishwashers, and 74 percent of janitors were native-born citizens. The figures show that American citizens are just as willing to assume these unskilled jobs.

In the economic downturn beginning in the last decade, manufacturers, using automated machinery, and other efficient and new technologies, have cut countless low-wage jobs. Manufacturers are also

Unskilled workers here recycle foul-smelling restaurant waste.

building factories in foreign countries and taking advantage of hiring workers in those countries that can produce goods more cheaply.

In 1950 the share of manufacturing jobs in the United States was at 33 percent. As of 2010, it had fallen to less than 10 percent. Unemployment rates are going up nearly twice as fast in cities and towns with large immigrant populations compared with unemployment rates in areas where there are fewer immigrants. Furthermore, wages in low immigration areas have increased by more than 40 percent over areas with high immigration. Each year since 2000, more than one million legal and illegal immigrants have settled in the country permanently, and the trend is expected to continue. Most will be low-wage earners who will displace native-born workers.

> **DID YOU KNOW?**
>
> According to the Department of Homeland Security, 9,359,479 people gained legal permanent residency status in the decade between 1998 and 2007.

Many immigrant families live near or at the poverty level. The poverty rate for immigrants and their children is 17 percent, almost twice that of native-born citizens. Many lower-income immigrant families rely on government assistance, such as food stamps, school lunch programs, unemployment benefits, Medicare, Medicaid, and aid to families with dependent children (AFDC), once called welfare. According to a report prepared by Stephen Camarota for the Center for Immigration Studies, 33 percent of immigrant families receive one or more of these services, compared with 19 percent of native-born families.

Immigrant families depending on income from low-wage jobs are not as likely as native-born citizens to carry health insurance. Without insurance, health care costs are too high for low-income families to afford basic medical care. Only when people become seriously ill or injured do they seek care, generally from a public clinic or a hospital emergency room. These costs are very expensive, and the burden of payment falls to the government and the taxpayers. A 2006 Census

Undocumented farmworkers line up to receive health care from a government-sponsored mobile clinic.

Bureau report stated that 43.8 percent of noncitizens are uninsured, compared with 12.7 percent of native-born citizens.

Immigrants impact the education system, and many believe that native-born citizens are penalized. In communities where immigration is high, the cost of educating immigrant children who do not speak English is also high. Many classrooms in heavily Latino neighborhoods are taught in both Spanish and English; teachers who are flu-

A public school teacher gives an English vocabulary lesson to Vietnamese-speaking students.

ent in two languages are paid higher salaries. A Federation for American Immigration Reform (FAIR) report estimates that, depending on class size, it costs $300 to $900 per year per student to provide dual-language classes. Native-born parents are often concerned that too much classroom time is taken up trying to engage and educate non–English speaking students. Students in higher education are also impacted by foreign-born students. Nearly 4 percent of university students are foreign born. In 2007 there were more than 80,000 university students from India and more than 75,000 from China. Many of these students are graduate students who also receive desirable employment as teaching and research assistants. Furthermore, states the Center for Immigration Studies, large numbers of foreign students lessen available opportunities for native-born women and minority students.

Professional Wage Earners

In the past two decades, middle-class workers and professional high-wage workers have also been adversely affected by immigrant competition, in particular, because of a visa program known as H-1B. This program allows highly trained foreign workers with particular skills (usually of a high-tech nature) to be employed by American companies in the United States when no qualified native-born citizens are available. This visa permits the workers to remain in the country for up to six years. During that time, however, these workers often find means of becoming permanent residents. According to the Code of Federal Regulations (CFR), the employer is required to hire the H-1B visa holder at a prevailing wage—in other words, at the same wage that would be paid to a U.S. citizen in the same job. In addition, employers must post all job listings publicly, and they may not fire American workers in order to hire H-1B workers.

There have been many abuses to the system, however. Many employers find ways to hire professionals from other countries and pay them lower wages than an American employee would receive. This practice leads to lower wages industry-wide and creates domestic unemployment. Senator Charles Grassley of Iowa, acknowledging that employers have sidestepped the rules in order to hire foreign-born workers at the expense of their American counterparts, said that he wants to close "loopholes that employers have exploited." He also acknowledged the "years of fraud and abuse," mainly in the technology employment sector. Critics of the program view it as a means for employers to import cheap labor.

Another visa program, the L-1 program, permits a visa holder to work in the United States for up to seven years if the worker had for a period of one year been employed overseas by an American company or a company at least partially controlled by an American firm. This visa program can also lead to permanent residency. Senator Richard Durbin of Illinois stated, "Our immigration policy should seek to complement our U.S. workforce, not replace it. Some employers have abused the H-1B and L-1 temporary work visa programs, using them to bypass qualified American job applicants." In response to widespread complaints,

Congress reduced the size of the H-1B program, though it permitted so many exemptions that displaced American professionals continued to be very angry. For example, there is no ceiling on the number of H-1B workers that can be hired by universities and by nonprofit hospitals and other organizations connected to colleges and universities. There are also no restrictions on hiring by nonprofit science or government research organizations.

Illegal Immigration

For many people, a big part of any discussion about immigration centers on illegal immigration. Data suggest that there are approximately 12 million illegal immigrants living in the United States and that 60 percent of them are from Mexico and Central America. It is difficult to be accurate about these numbers because illegal residents do not respond to census surveys nor do they reveal any information that would jeopardize their presence in the United States.

Illegal immigration touches people and communities in countless ways. Often, illegal aliens who work do not pay taxes. Many employ-

DID YOU KNOW?

There are 140,000 employment-based permanent worker visas, and 28.6 percent are granted to Priority One workers: i.e., persons with extraordinary ability and international acclaim; outstanding professors and researchers; and executives of multinational corporations.

ees use false identification to obtain jobs, while others are simply hired and paid off the books. Illegal immigrants who work for an employer and provide false information about their identity are called **undocumented workers**. The undocumented workers and their employers do not pay payroll taxes, as the illegal workers are hidden from taxing authorities. Furthermore, employers of low-wage workers who suspect that they are hiring illegal aliens or are knowingly doing so pay wages that are much lower than they would pay a citizen or legal resident doing the same work. The Center for Immigration Studies (CIS) says that 57 percent of illegal aliens come from Mexico and that the "typical Mexican worker earns one-tenth his American counterpart, and numerous American businesses are willing to hire cheap, compliant labor from abroad." The CIS study goes on to say that illegal immigrants help and encourage their friends and family members to also enter the country illegally, a situation that increases the drag on wages and the competition with legal citizens for jobs.

Illegal immigrants place an undue burden on public education. A 1982 Supreme Court ruling, *Plyler v. Doe*, stated that every child, whether in the United States legally or not, is to be given access to a free public education. It is estimated that there are 3 million children of illegal immigrants who attend public school in the United States. The Federation for Immigration Reform reported that the cost of educating these children is as high as $28 billion each year. Some contend that the parents who work illegally do not pay enough taxes to support the extra funds that schools spend to educate their children. In some states

Many local, state, and national politicians recognize that immigration reform is a divisive and complex issue. Here, protestors demand action from lawmakers in Washington, D.C.

where illegal immigration is high, schools cut back on expenses by laying off teachers, purchasing fewer textbooks, increasing class sizes, and discontinuing sports programs and other after-school activities.

The Pew Hispanic Center said in a report, "A growing number believe that immigrants are a burden to the country, taking jobs and housing and creating strains on the health care system." Americans also have concerns about illegal immigrants and law enforcement. According to the Department of Homeland Security's *2008 Yearbook of Immigration Statistics*, more than 200,000 illegal aliens were imprisoned in 2008 for committing crimes such as theft, burglary, assault, and murder, and many of them were later deported. The yearbook also cites another 550,000 illegal immigrants who were deported for violating immigration laws; illegally entering the country *is* a federal crime.

At the forefront of any discussion of illegal aliens and crime is terrorism and national security. The attacks on the World Trade Center in New York City in 1993 and in 2001 were largely perpetrated by persons in the country illegally. Mostly all of the pilots who hijacked the airplanes in 2001 were illegal aliens. According to the Census Bureau, there are tens of thousands of illegal aliens living in the United States who are from countries who support anti-American terrorism.

> # DID YOU KNOW?
> On April 23, 2010, Jan Brewer, the governor of Arizona, signed the Support Our Law Enforcement and Safe Neighborhoods Act, a set of strict anti-immigration laws giving police more authority to ask for proof of legal immigration status.

English

President Theodore Roosevelt said, "We have room for but one language here, and that is the English language. . . ." Historically, immigrants arrived in the United States and eagerly set out to learn English. Speaking a common language helped newcomers understand the ways and the laws of their newly adopted country, as well as enabling them to find better jobs or to attend school. Today one in five persons in the United States speaks a language other than English at home according to the U.S. Census Bureau, and only a little more than half speak English well. On August 11, 2000, President Clinton signed Executive Order 13166, called the Improving Access to Services for Persons with Limited English Proficiency. The order, which expanded the scope of Title VI of the 1964 Civil Rights Act, states that "each Federal agency shall examine the services it provides and develop and implement a system by which LEP (Limited English Proficiency) persons can meaningfully access those services consistent with, and without unduly burdening, the fundamental mission of the agency." In plain English, federal agencies and other public agencies that receive federal funds, grants, or subsidies must provide translations of their materials and services in the native languages of non-English speaking persons. Included in this order are libraries, transportation departments, parks, schools, public health clinics, courts, welfare and unemployment offices, and other social service agencies. There are 231 languages spoken in the United States, and more than 6,000 languages spoken throughout the world. Executive Order 13166 could theoretically apply to hundreds of languages. (This executive order applies only to languages spoken in the U.S.—not the world.) Costs for translations and translators rise yearly, while at the same time the recession economy has put even greater financial demands on public services.

Many believe that English should be declared the official language of the U.S. government. Since the enactment of Executive Order 13166, bills in both the House of Representatives and the Senate have been proposed with the goal of repealing it. According to Senator James Inhofe of Oklahoma, who proposed such a bill in May 2009, 72 percent to 83 percent of Americans support English as the official language of government. There is evidence suggesting that immigrants do not really benefit from Executive Order 13166. When students participate in bilingual education, for example, they do not feel pressure to learn English quickly or with proficiency. In addition, workers with limited English skills have difficulty communicating with customers, employers, and coworkers. Furthermore, translations are not always reliable or available.

WHAT DO YOU THINK?

Do you think English lessons for non–English speaking students in public schools should be paid for by taxpayers?

Do you think that local communities and/or states should have the authority to pass immigration legislation that is suitable to their situation?

How would you compare many Americans' attitudes toward Irish immigrants in the nineteenth century with their attitudes toward Mexican immigrants in the twentieth and twenty-first centuries?

Do you think the cost of social services expenditures is balanced by the productivity of low-wage immigrant workers?

Chapter 3

In New York Harbor, the Statue of Liberty stands at the "golden door," as her torch "glows worldwide welcome. . . ." For centuries, people from all over the world have come to America seeking liberties in the forms of religious freedom, political and legal rights, better education, social parity, and economic advancement. In the first waves of immigration, the new arrivals stepped on American soil to work hard, to learn a new way of life, and in most cases to accept and cooperate with the cultural differences of others. As immigrants developed and prospered, their children attended school and entered into the mainstream of American life, bringing with them, and sharing with others, their parents' work ethic, cultural traditions, and values. One has only to look at the richness of American life to see their influences—in food traditions, music, literature, art, religion, holidays and celebrations, entrepreneurial ingenuity, scientific discovery, political and social ideals, and educational practices.

Economy

Many immigrants who have come to America have had considerable drive and ambition. Rejecting the status quo in their native countries,

The Latino population is growing by 40 percent a year, becoming a major influence on American society.

The diversity of America gave rise to jazz, a purely American music form, which is a combination of music from Africa, Cuba, Spain, and South and Central America.

whether economic, social, or political, they sought a life that offered freedom, prosperity, and a better chance of success and equality for their children.

People who wish to limit immigration often claim that immigrants take jobs away from native-born citizens and negatively impact the lives of native-born low-wage earners. However, those who favor immigration point to data and reports from numerous sources that reject these claims. Writing in the *Bulletin for Free Trade*, Daniel Griswold offered a counterclaim: while low-skilled, foreign-born workers may affect wages, the immigrant workers add more to the economy than they take in return. "The arrival of low-skilled, foreign-born

DID YOU KNOW?

In 2009, there were more than 650,000 international students enrolled in U.S. colleges and universities. They paid nearly $18 billion in tuition and other education-related expenses.

workers in the labor force increases the incentives for younger native-born Americans to stay in school and for older workers to upgrade their skills" and advance upwardly in the labor force. Thus, he says, they do not compete with foreign-born workers.

The idea of immigrants encouraging native-born citizens to stay in school is not a new one. A paper published by the National Bureau of Economic Research recounts "the high school movement" of the period 1910–1940. At the time, there was a large wave of immigrants from eastern and southern Europe who assumed many low-wage jobs in America. Meanwhile, during that same period, the percentage of native-born eighteen-year-olds who graduated from high school rose

Scholarships and education grants are often limited to citizens only. Legal immigrant students are often older learners who have adult responsibilities and families to support, so supporters want legal permanent residents to have the chance to apply for financial aid to attend college.

from under 10 percent to more than 50 percent. John Gay, of the American Hotel and Lodging Association, holds a similar belief, as quoted in *USA Today*: "There are places in this country where we wouldn't survive without immigrants. . . . The trend is to push our own children into college to be rocket scientists or computer programmers. But who is going to do these hard jobs that we have?" In a 2002 *Wall Street Journal* article, Tamar Jacoby, president of Immigration Works USA, said that Americans are growing more educated. She says that only 10 percent of native-born males drop out of high school to look for unskilled work, compared with 50 percent in 1960.

Fewer native-born workers apply for low-wage jobs when they have lost better-paying jobs. Native-born workers are also much less likely

Migrant farm workers on the West Coast follow harvests from California to Washington State.

to uproot themselves and move elsewhere to look for work. Immigrant low-wage workers, on the other hand, are more flexible and will travel anywhere for work; for example, they seek jobs in chicken-processing factories in Arkansas and meatpacking plants in Kansas, they pick cherries in Washington State and harvest grapes in California, they build retirement-homes in Arizona, and they work as kitchen help and in maid service in Florida hotels. Although this employment pattern is tied to the economy to some degree, especially in construction, there is usually a consistent demand for immigrant workers in agriculture, food processing, home health care, and seasonal work at resort and vacation areas. In the recession during the first decade of the 2000s, many mills and factories with an immigrant labor force slowed their production, and immigration also decreased. Jacoby states that native-born workers tend to "cluster at the middle rungs of the economic ladder," and that immigrants are more likely found at the lower and upper rungs. "By and large," he writes, "newcomers complement rather than compete with those already here."

Taxes and Government Benefits

Many of those opposed to immigration claim that immigrants take more from the government than they give back. Some refute this claim. One representative from the Social Security Administration (SSA) said that immigration helps the system "remain solvent." He admits that in its financial planning, the SSA relies on immigrants' contributions to Social Security taxes. The average age of Americans is becoming older, as the baby boom generation (those born after World War II in the years from 1946 to 1964) retires from the workforce and collects Social Security payments. The baby boom generation did not produce enough children and thus new workers, who would now be paying into the Social Security system. The millions of baby boom retirees are having an enormous impact on the ability of the Social Security system to pay their benefits. More new and younger workers are needed. Retirees benefit from the taxes that immigrant workers contribute. The National Research Council reports that the nation's 34 million immigrants pay more in taxes than they consume in public services and benefits. Most of them work and pay federal, state, and local taxes. Furthermore, the report has found that many immigrants, once near retirement age, return to their home countries and do not ever claim American Social Security or Medicare benefits.

A new employee provides his "green card" and Social Security paperwork to his employer.

"GREEN CARD" SOLDIERS

The military is developing a program to recruit noncitizens into active-duty service. Immigrants holding green cards have always been eligible to enlist in the military. Today, however, there is a new effort that will allow temporary immigrants, including students and refugees, to enlist if they have lived in the United States for a minimum of two years. In 2010 it was estimated that there were 30,000 to 40,000 noncitizen service members in the military. Armed forces recruiters want to attract temporary immigrants with foreign language skills, post-high school educations, and professional expertise. There is a shortage in the military of doctors, nurses, interpreters, translators, and people who have native knowledge about foreign cultures. The army particularly wants to attract people who speak Arabic, Chinese, Pashto, Hindi, Igbo (a Nigerian language), Kurdish, Russian, and Tamil. As one army official pointed out, "The American Army finds itself in a lot of different countries where cultural awareness is critical."

Some people worry that the new noncitizen recruits may have stronger ties to their native countries than to the United States or that the program opens the way for terrorists to infiltrate the military. However, the U.S. Citizenship and Immigration Service very carefully investigates noncitizens before they enlist. Furthermore, the United States has had a long tradition of accepting noncitizens into the military, beginning with the Revolutionary War and continuing through both world wars

Enlisting in the military can be a path to citizenship for many immigrants.

and the Vietnam War. Many noncitizen soldiers have attained distinction. Mexican-born Alfred Rascon, an undocumented immigrant soldier, received the Congressional Medal of Honor and later became the director of the Selective Service System, and General John Shalikashvili, a Polish-born immigrant, served in the U.S. military and was appointed chairman of the Joint Chiefs of Staff by President Clinton.

Immigration detractors assert that there is a high cost of crime associated with immigrants. In testimony before Congress in 2007, however, Professor Anne Piehl of Rutgers University used census data to support her claim that immigrants are imprisoned for crimes at one-fifth the rate of native-born citizens. Professor Ruben Rumbaut of the University of California also used census data to show that immigrants without high school diplomas had an incarceration rate that was one-fourth that of native-born high school graduates and one-seventh that of native-born citizens who did not graduate from high school. Immigration authorities have long asserted that they screen immigrants for any criminal history before they are admitted to the United States and turn people away if there is any evidence of wrongdoing. These sources support the view that immigrants come to America to pursue opportunity and do not want to compromise their ambition by breaking any laws or committing crimes.

Immigrant workers stimulate the economy in many ways. According to the Selig Center for Economic Growth at the University of Georgia, in 2008 foreign-born consumers purchased more than 14 percent of the nation's goods and services, and that total reached $1.5 trillion. These purchases provided state and local governments with sales tax income. A National Academy of Sciences study found that an average immigrant and his or her children will pay $80,000 more in taxes than they ever would collect in government services. For immigrants with high-wage professions, the taxes they pay over the period of their careers amount to $200,000 or more.

Professional Immigrant Workers

Much has been said, particularly in the academic and high-technology fields, that immigrants are displacing qualified American students and professionals. About one in three immigrants has a college degree, and among them, 42 percent hold master's, professional, or doctorate degrees compared with 36 percent of college-educated, native-born citizens. These individuals have made major contributions to America's success, especially in mathematics, science, medicine, and high technology. A recent Duke University study showed that in the past decade, immigrants founded 25 percent of all new American engineer-

Nobel Prize–winning scientist Albert Einstein, seen here taking his oath of United States citizenship, was an emigrant from Germany. He later warned the U.S. government during World War II that Germany was developing an atomic bomb.

ing and technology companies. Immigrants were also listed as inventors or coinventors of 24 percent of all international patents in 2006. Many recognize that the best way to compete in the global economy is to keep the "best and the brightest" foreign-born students in the United States rather than send them home. Foreign-born students and professionals bring knowledge about the advances in science, medicine, and technology of their home countries. In addition, they provide valuable academic and business relationships with colleagues from their native countries.

DID YOU KNOW?

Reflecting the recession, employers' requests for H-1B visas for highly skilled workers has decreased. In years past, the 65,000 visa cap was reached in a few days. In 2010, the cap was not reached for nearly a year.

Illegal Immigration

Illegal immigration is a problem in this country and a dilemma for politicians and the public alike. First and foremost, illegal immigrants live a life "in the shadows," and while they work and support their families, in many states they are ineligible for the rights and benefits available to legal residents and citizens. A majority of the approximately 12 million illegal immigrants work; they make up nearly 5 percent of the country's labor force. Some work off the books and so do not pay payroll taxes. Others supply employers with false identification. With false identification, employers deduct payroll taxes from the workers' paychecks and forward them to the government. Internal Revenue Service spokespeople say that the illegal workers' taxes are "free money."

Undocumented workers gather along a street hoping to be hired as day laborers in construction, landscaping, or any other odd jobs.

The money is collected but cannot be returned to the illegal workers in the form of tax refunds, Social Security, or other government payments. It has been claimed that billions of dollars each year are collected from illegal immigrants' paychecks, $9 billion to Social Security alone. Many of the illegal workers who pay taxes are low-wage earners who would otherwise be eligible for tax refunds. However, as they are undocumented workers, they cannot come forth to receive a refund. The tax money collected from undocumented workers earns the government an extra $6 billion to $7 billion in Social Security tax revenue and $1.5 billion in Medicare taxes each year. Economist William Ford commented, "The real question is how many of them pay more than they owe." Besides many paying state, local, and federal taxes through their paychecks, all illegal immigrants are consumers who pay sales tax with every purchase.

The fact that illegal immigrants cannot be open about their residency has other consequences. Not only do they work for lower wages, but they also do not receive employers' benefits such as unemployment compensation, health insurance, protection under the law against discrimination, overtime pay, and occupational safety. Many employers turn a blind eye to the status of their illegal employees as their profits increase when they hire people for less money. Likewise, many average American citizens also take advantage of illegal workers. As Robert Scheer wrote in the *San Francisco Chronicle,* people complain about the "waves" of immigrants flowing through the borders, yet "most Americans are quite happy to eat the food harvested by those same harassed and abused workers as well as entrusting the 'illegals' with the care of American homes and children." Many who are concerned about the treatment of illegal workers would like to see a change in immigration policy so that illegal immigrants could be granted amnesty or be given the means to become legal residents. Jose Millan, California's labor commissioner, said, "I am in favor of anything that brings these workers out of the shadows and into the sunlight; it's very easy to exploit a population when they're afraid. We would be a better country if we recognized the fact that there are 10 million undocumented workers in our midst, and we would be better off if they were granted the benefits and responsibilities of a legal existence."

DID YOU KNOW?

A Center for Immigration Studies report estimated that it would cost between $206 billion and $230 billion over five years to deport all illegal immigrants.

WHAT DO YOU THINK?

To what extent do you feel that employers should investigate the immigration status of their workers?

Do you feel that there is a balance between what American citizens gain from work performed by illegal immigrants and what they lose in job opportunities?

Do you think that the number of skilled workers and college students who request visas are affected by changes in the U.S. economy?

Do you think the economic growth of China and India will have an effect on the number of people wanting to immigrate to the United States?

Chapter 4

Some people on both sides of the immigration debate find themselves in agreement on one thing: that government policies regarding immigration should be reexamined. In their view, both illegal and legal immigration lie at the root of serious social and economic problems. Others, however, contend that immigration laws shortchange immigrants, businesses, and society. Concerns about the threat of terrorism have increased recognition of the *need* for significant reform but not what form it should take.

The government is responsible for patrolling the nation's borders and overseeing the people who enter the country. It is also responsible for maintaining contact with legal immigrants and visa holders while they are visiting or residing in the country and for deporting any individuals who are living in the country illegally.

Patrolling Borders

The U.S. Customs and Border Protection (CBP) is part of the Department of Homeland Security. The CBP agency responsible for actively defending the physical borders is the U.S. Border Patrol. Border patrol agents are charged with preventing terrorists and dangerous weapons from

A boy waves an American flag at a pro-immigration rally in Washington, D.C.

entering the United States and detecting and detaining anyone trying to enter the country illegally. In 2009 approximately 20,000 border patrol agents were guarding the 3,987-mile (6,416-km) border with Canada and the 1,952-mile (3,141-km) border with Mexico. They also patrol waters around Puerto Rico and Florida and the maritime boundaries with Cana-

A Border Patrol agent has the lonely and sometimes very dangerous task of watching for illegal activity in the vast desert along the southwestern U.S.–Mexican border.

The cost of catching illegal immigrants is rising rapidly. The bill for patrolling the borders has risen from $326 million in 1992 to $2.7 billion in 2010.

da. In a stepped-up effort to reduce illegal immigration and intercept terrorists, much of the Border Patrol's attention is paid to the Mexico–U.S. border, where most illegal immigration to the United States occurs. The DHS wants to spend $3 million to $4 million per mile to build a high-tech wall between the two countries. Besides the desire to detain and turn back illegal Mexican and other Latin American immigrants, officials believe they can also capture terrorists. Said one DHS representative,

"Several al-Qaeda leaders believe operatives can pay their way into the country through Mexico." Despite possible threats to national

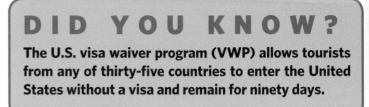

DID YOU KNOW?

The U.S. visa waiver program (VWP) allows tourists from any of thirty-five countries to enter the United States without a visa and remain for ninety days.

security, there are many people who are opposed to the enormous cost of constructing a wall to catch a few, if any, terrorists, who may also be arriving from other points of entry: by air, by ship, or from Canada, where there are far fewer agents guarding a much longer border.

Overseeing People

The USCIS is an agency under the CBP that is responsible for overseeing legal immigrant applications for permanent residency, citizenship, education, or employment. It also reviews and determines eligibility for nonimmigrant visas. For many of these visas, the USCIS requires that an immigrant have a sponsor, either a family member or an employer. Most categories of visas have annual quotas, although a family category called "immediate relative" does not have a quota attached.

DID YOU KNOW?

The test to become a naturalized citizen of the United States has one hundred possible questions covering three subject areas: American history, American government, and civics. To pass, a person must correctly answer six out of ten questions.

An immediate relative is often a spouse, child, or the parent of a legal U.S. citizen over twenty-one years of age. However, the rule specifically prevents a child under age twenty one, born in the United States and and therefore a U.S. citizen, from sponsoring his or her illegal parents.

The application process is expensive and may take months or years, depending upon quotas and the applicant's family category and native country. Although quotas based on nationality were abolished in the Immigration and Naturalization Act of 1965, there remains a 7 percent cap on the total of number of visas available to applicants from any one country, no matter the type of visa. As there are many more applicants from Mexico, India, and China than from countries in South America and Africa, many consider this system unfair and a reason for reform.

For an employer-sponsored visa, the applicant must have a job already established. Though work visas are temporary, the visa holder may marry and eventually acquire permanent resident status. The H-1B visa is for highly skilled professional workers that many high-tech businesses are anxious to hire. Companies such as Microsoft and Verizon advocate higher quotas for these types of workers. An H-2B visa is for low-wage nonagricultural temporary work; these visa holders find jobs at ski resorts, hotels, and restaurants and as landscapers and construction workers. The USCIS also issues nonimmigrant student visas, which have no quotas.

Government quota policies are challenged by people on both sides of the debate. Some believe that the quotas are too large, and

U.S. immigration policies have torn many immigrant families apart, separating illegal immigrant parents from their U.S.–born children.

others believe that the quotas are too small. On one side, employers and many politicians want to see the quotas expanded. Employers of high-wage professionals want to hire worldly, well-educated experts who can help them compete globally. Employers of low-wage workers want the economic advantage of paying lower wages to persons willing to work difficult jobs. Furthermore, many people express the belief that increased quotas would decrease illegal immigration, and many decry that family-sponsored immigrant quotas unnecessarily tear families apart. Politicians hear from a growing population of Latino immigrant voters in the United States who plead for legal immigration for their family members. There are also many who believe the opposite: that American immigration quotas are too generous. Those concerned say that too many immigrants create a lower standard of living for all by encouraging lower wages and putting undue pressure on finite natural resources, fossil fuels, and energy consumption.

Immigration Enforcement

The **U.S. Immigration and Customs Enforcement (ICE)** is the agency that enforces customs and immigration laws. The ICE is the largest enforcement and investigative agency under the DHS, and it has grown ever larger in the aftermath of the terrorist attacks of September 2001. Nineteen terrorists involved in the attacks were in the country on temporary or expired student or tourist visas. Learning of this lack of oversight, government lawmakers responded by establishing the cabinet-level Department of Homeland Security to increase enforcement of interior immigration policies such as investigating and deporting illegal workers, persons with expired visas, and legal and illegal immigrants who have committed crimes.

The ICE's courts and prisons have become overwhelmed with detainees. Many of the detainees are illegal Latin American immigrants and often their families. The prisons were designed to house criminals

An upgraded ICE detention cell designed for families.

and not people who do not threaten the nation's security. In the spring of 2009 there was a backlog of more than 200,000 persons waiting to appear before an immigration judge. Trials can take months or years to be completed. The ICE detainees are not given parole. As a result, immigration jails are overcrowded. In 2009 the DHS secretary, Janet Napolitano, announced that the government would overhaul the ICE system: "We are improving detention center management to prioritize health, safety and uniformity among our facilities while ensuring security, efficiency and fiscal responsibility."

Illegal Immigration

Illegal immigration is a huge part of the discussion for immigration reform. Although illegal immigrants live in an "underworld" hidden from view, they can directly affect the lives of legal residents and citizens. Many Americans want to see enforcement officials increase their scrutiny of the illegal immigrant population, and they want to see more arrests and more deportations.

For many years, illegal immigrants from Mexico crossed the border to do seasonal and labor-intensive agriculture work, such as planting and harvesting. Farmers and the government usually turned a blind eye to this practice. A new problem arose in the 1980s, when American companies built large manufacturing plants, called *maquiladoras*, on the Mexican side of the border in order to take advantage of the cheap Mexican labor. However, the companies decided wages were still too high and moved their operations to other countries in Central America or Asia. The Mexican workers, who had become accustomed to a better standard of living, began illegally crossing the border in greater numbers to look for work in nonagricultural jobs. The Immigration Reform and Control Act of 1986 required employers to refuse to give jobs to illegal immigrants or pay a fine. Millions of dollars in fines were collected in the early years after the law passed, but the fines have grown smaller since 1992.

The ICE has recently been stepping up raids on businesses known to have undocumented employees. Armed with a civil search warrant, the ICE agents make surprise sweeps through factories and farms to in-

A Coca-Cola bottling plant uses E-verify to ensure that its workers have the legal right to work.

vestigate workers' documents and arrest those who have provided false identification. Most of the undocumented workers are deported quickly in order to avoid the expense of prison and court costs. Both employers and advocates for illegal workers are angry. Though employers seem to escape heavy fines, they still find themselves without the workers they had depended on. Advocates for immigrants condemn the ICE actions as they see families separated, their livelihoods destroyed, and hundreds of hardworking community members deported.

Starting late in the first decade of the 2000s, government officials have been moving the focus away from illegal employees and directing their attention to employers who hire undocumented workers. There is much discussion over the fines. If they are too low, employers will consider the fines a cost of doing business. If the fines are too high, many fear that the businesses will close and move their operations out of the country.

Those demanding immigration reform agree that employers must have the means to double-check identification papers. A program called E-Verify is a new system that allows employers to check the Social Security database for legitimate Social Security numbers.

Many support the idea that illegal workers should be

DID YOU KNOW?

E-Verify is currently used by more than 180,000 employers at approximately 675,000 work sites.

granted the means of becoming legal residents. It has been proposed by several legislators and President Obama that there should be a path to citizenship. Deporting 12 million illegal immigrants is not a viable solution in the eyes of many. One solution for the people already here is for them to earn their legal status by paying a fine, learning English, and "stepping to the back of the line" in the backlog of people with legal visas who are waiting for their immigration papers to be processed. In calling for comprehensive reform, Interior Secretary Ken Salazar said, "We need to have laws in place to take us from today's chaos and lawlessness to law and order. That law and order system must include: increased border security, strict enforcement of immigration laws including a sound employer verification system and a realistic method of dealing with the human and economic reality of millions of undocumented workers in America."

That everything about immigration is in need of reform of one sort or another is widely agreed upon. Has the conventional notion of the United States as a nation of immigrants outlived its usefulness? There are economic arguments both for and against immigration—also disagreements about the number of immigrants granted entry—as well as calls from both sides for a restructuring of the visa classifications in the quota system. Ultimately the question is, "Who gets to be an American?"

WHAT DO YOU THINK?

Do you think the United States has benefited from immigration? Does it still? Why or why not?

What do you think about the quota system? Is it appropriate? Is it fair?

What do you know about the criteria for naturalized citizenship? Do you agree with the current rules?

In 1883, the poet Emma Lazarus wrote the poem entitled "The Great Colossus." It was inscribed in bronze and placed at the base of the Statue of Liberty in New York Harbor. The final verse reads,

> **"Keep, ancient lands, your storied pomp!" cries she**
> **With silent lips. "Give me your tired, your poor,**
> **Your huddled masses yearning to breathe free,**
> **The wretched refuse of your teeming shore.**

Send these, the homeless, tempest-tossed to me,
I lift my lamp beside the golden door!"

What relationship does the poem have to policies and attitudes of immigration in the twenty-first century? If you were to rewrite the verse, what might you say?

CERTIFICATES AND VISAS

There are several certificates and visas that apply to immigrants to the United States. Certificates are official documents of legal immigration and **nonimmigrant** status. A visa is a stamp that is attached to an immigrant's **passport**. The immigrant must apply for a visa at an American embassy or consulate in his or her native country. There are many kinds of visas, but none of them can be obtained in the United States.

A **B-1 Business Visa** is issued to persons who come to the United States for business purposes for a period no longer than six months. A person with a B-1 visa cannot accept a salary or payment of any kind.

A **B-2 Tourist Visa** is given to people who plan to visit the United States. Persons are allowed to stay for up to six months. Some tourists may stay without a visa for up to ninety days if their country is one of thirty-

Citizens of foreign countries can apply for either temporary or permanent visas. A visitor visa, shown here, is a nonimmigrant visa that gives permission to foreign citizens to enter the U.S. temporarily for business, tourism, or medical treatment.

five countries that are part of a visa waiver program; included are Australia, France, Switzerland, Singapore, Sweden, and the United Kingdom.

A **B-2 Visa for Medical Treatment** allows a person with acceptable documentation from a physician to enter the country for medical treatment.

An **F-1 Student Visa** is given to full-time students who wish to study in American high schools, universities, and other institutions of higher education. Students may remain in the United States for as long as they are enrolled in a full-time academic program.

An **H-1B Work Visa** is a nonimmigrant visa that allows a person with a college education or a "specialty occupation" to work temporarily in the United States for up to six years. An employer is not allowed to replace an American worker with an H-1B worker or to pay him or her less than an American would be paid to do the same work. Typical occupations include accountants, high-technology workers, engineers, financial analysts, health care workers, scientists, and lawyers. The employers must sponsor the worker.

An **H-2B Work Visa** is a nonimmigrant visa given to a temporary or seasonal nonagricultural worker. Jobs can be skilled or unskilled, and the worker must be sponsored by the employer. Types of jobs include restaurant workers, house-keepers and janitors, retail salespeople, lifeguards, ski lift operators, golf course personnel, and grounds keepers. When the job ends, the worker must return home.

A **J-1 Exchange Visa** is a visa that applies to person who comes to the United States for a short period of time to be a student, visiting scholar, trainee, au pair (nanny), teacher, professor, research assistant, doctor, or researcher or to participate in a cultural exchange program.

A **K-1 Fiancée and Fiancé Visa** is a temporary visa given to a person who plans to marry a U.S. citizen. The marriage must take place within ninety days. The new spouse does not become a naturalized citizen until after he or she applies for and receives a green card through marriage certificate.

A **K-2 Visa** is a visa given to the minor children of a K-1 visa holder.

A **U-Visa** is a visa given to a foreigner who has been the victim of a crime and who is willing to assist U.S. law enforcement in convicting the criminal or criminals responsible.

Dual Citizenship

Some people become citizens of two countries. For example, a child born in the United States to foreign parents or a child born to U.S. citizens living in a foreign country. **Dual citizenship** requires a person to obey the laws of both countries, pay taxes, and serve in the military if necessary.

Certificate of Citizenship

An immigrant must apply for citizenship, and if accepted, a certification of citizenship is issued by the USCIS. The document gives a person all the rights of citizenship, including the right to vote, hold a government job, run for public office (although not president or vice president), sponsor foreign family members as immigrants, carry a U.S. passport, and receive Social Security, Medicare, and other public benefits. Children under eighteen whose parents have a certificate of citizenship generally become citizens automatically.

An immigrant woman has just participated in a naturalization ceremony and proudly holds her certificate of American citizenship.

Certificate of Naturalization

A Certificate of Naturalization is a document issued by the USCIS to an immigrant who was not born in the United States nor born to a U.S. citizen. To qualify, an immigrant must pass literacy and civics tests and take an oath to the United States.

Certificate of Asylum or Refugee Status

Persons in fear of persecution in their native country on the basis of their race, religion, nationality, membership in a particular social group, or political beliefs can apply for asylum or refugee status. To apply for refugee status, persons must be living outside the United States. To apply for asylum, persons must be living in the United States or apply at a port of entry. After being granted asylum or refugee status, an immigrant who has lived in the country for one year can apply for a green card.

Permanent Resident Card (Green Card)

A Permanent Resident card, known as a green card, is an identification card stating that a person can legally live in the United States permanently. The card is proof that a person is registered with the USCIS. A green card holder may also travel outside the United States for up to one year at a time, sponsor a green card for a family member, and apply for citizenship after a certain number of years.

Diversity Immigrant Visa Program (Green Card Lottery)

The USCIS issues 55,000 Permanent Resident Cards each year by lottery through the Diversity Immigrant Visa Program, commonly known as the Green Card Lottery. Only people from countries that have sent fewer than 50,000 immigrants to the United States are eligible. Of the more than 12 million people who enter the lottery, approximately 100,000 are randomly selected by computer. Those selected and their family members may apply for permanent-resident status.

Glossary

alien—A foreign-born person who has not become a naturalized citizen of the country in which he or she resides.

amnesty—An official pardon granted to a large group of individuals.

asylum—A protected status: in particular, the status sought by someone in a country not his or her own, on grounds of persecution because of race, religion, nationality, political associations or affiliations, or similar causes.

Department of Homeland Security (DHS)—A cabinet department of the U.S. government. It is responsible for responding to natural disasters and protecting the United States from terrorist or other attacks.

deport—To send an alien back to his or her own country of origin, usually in response to criminal activity or violation of immigration laws.

dual citizenship—The condition of being a citizen of two countries, with the requirement of obeying the laws of each.

green card—The popular name for the Permanent Resident Card (formerly the Alien Registration Receipt Card) issued by the U.S. government.

immigrant—A foreign-born person who takes up residence in another country.

naturalized citizen—A foreign-born person who has become a citizen and is granted all the rights of a citizen, except the right to become president or vice president of the United States.

nonimmigrant—A person who is temporarily in a country other than his or her own, often for a specific purpose.

passport—A travel document that shows the bearer's origin, identity, and nationality and allows entrance into a foreign country.

Permanent Resident Card—Identification issued by the U.S. Customs and Immigration Service that grants permanent residence in the United States.

quota—A fixed number or percentage.

refugee—A person who flees for safety to another country, fearing persecution in his or her country of origin because of race, religion, nationality, membership in a particular social group, or political opinion. A person must be living outside the United States when requesting refugee status.

undocumented worker—A person who is employed without having valid identification and legal permission to work.

U.S. Immigration and Customs Enforcement (ICE)—Part of the DHS that is responsible for investigating and enforcing immigration and detaining and deporting violators.

visa—A stamp placed on a passport by the proper authority that allows temporary entry into a country. To enter the United States, the visa must be issued by a consulate outside the United States.

Find Out More

Books

Bial, Raymond. *Ellis Island: Coming to the Land of Liberty*. Boston: Houghton Mifflin Books for Children, 2009.

Flanagan, Alice K. *Angel Island*. Minneapolis, MN: Compass Point Books, 2006.

Kenney, Karen Latchana. *Illegal Immigration*. Edina, MN: ABDO Publishing, 2008.

Lansford, Tom, ed. *Immigration*. Detroit: Greenhaven Press, 2009.

Stefoff, Rebecca. *A Century of Immigration: 1820–1924*. New York: Marshall Cavendish Benchmark, 2007.

Wilson, Ruth. *Immigration*. North Mankato, MN: Stargazer Books, 2008.

Websites

Center for Immigration Studies
www.cis.org/

Department of Homeland Security Yearbook of Immigration Statistics
www.dhs.gov/files/statistics/publications/yearbook.shtm

Federation for Immigration Reform
www.fairus.org/

Immigration Works USA
www.immigrationworksusa.org/

New York Times Immigration Interactive map
www.nytimes.com/interactive/2009/03/10/us/20090310-immigration-explorer.html

U.S. Customs and Border Protection

www.cbp.gov/

U.S. Immigration and Customs Enforcement

www.ice.gov/

Organizations

U.S. Census Bureau

Public Information Office

4700 Silver Hill Road

Washington, D.C. 20233

800-923-8282

www.census.gov/

U.S. Citizenship and Immigration Services (USCIS)

Information and Customer Service Division MS 2260

111 Massachusetts Avenue NW

Washington, D.C. 20529-2260

800-375-5283

www.uscis.gov/

U.S. Department of Homeland Security (DHS)

Washington, D.C. 20528

202-282-8000

www.dhs.gov/

Index
Page numbers in boldface are illustrations.

About the Author

Ruth Bjorklund lives on Bainbridge Island across Puget Sound from Seattle, Washington. She has written numerous books for young people and hopes that this book will help students explore the complex topic of immigration in the United States.